I'm Reading About

NEW YORK

The Empire State

GALLOPADE

by Carole Marsh

Printed and Manufactured in Peachtree City, GA., USA
www.gallopade.com

Book design: John Hanson

Editorial manager: Janice Baker

New York is a great state.

It is one of a kind.

What makes New York special?

Let's read about it

and see!

NATIVE AMERICANS

Who lived in New York first?

Native Americans did!

They moved around to find food.
They hunted in New York's woods.
They fished in New York's rivers.
They gathered fruits and seeds and nuts.

EXPLORERS

The first explorers came to New York in 1524.
They came from the country of France.

Giovanni da Verrazzano was their leader.
He and his men were looking for
a quicker way to get to Asia!

SETTLEMENT

A group of people came from the Netherlands to America. They started the first settlement in New York. They named it New Amsterdam.

New York was one of the original 13 colonies.

New Amsterdam
New Amsterdam

STATEHOOD

New York was the 11th state
to join the United States of America!

Isn't it great,
to be a state!
I bet New York
could hardly wait!

New York became a state in 1788.

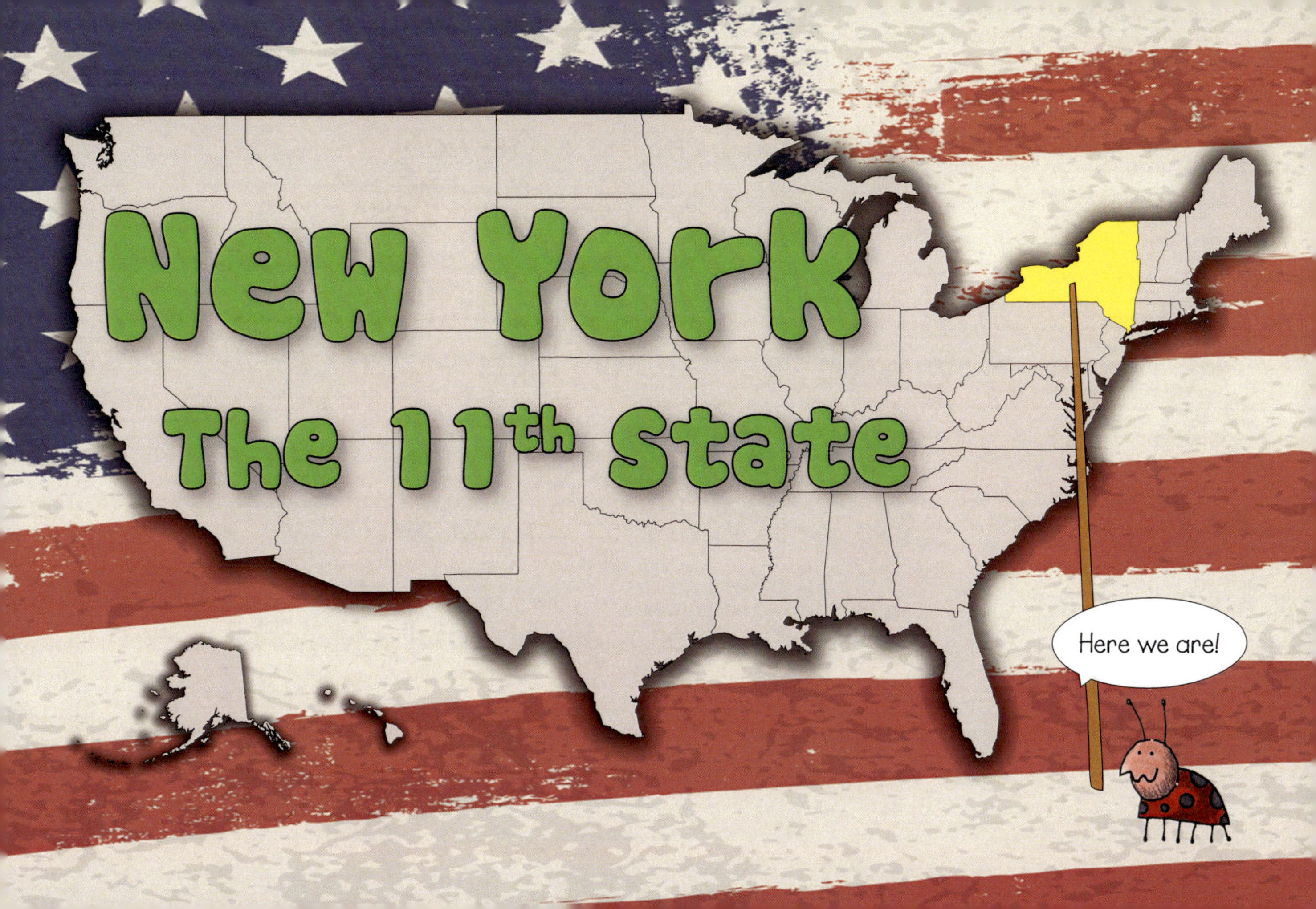
New York
The 11th State
Here we are!

FLAG

I am the state flag.
I was adopted in 1788.

What color am I?
I am blue.

Look at me.
What else do you see?

I fly high over the state of New York!

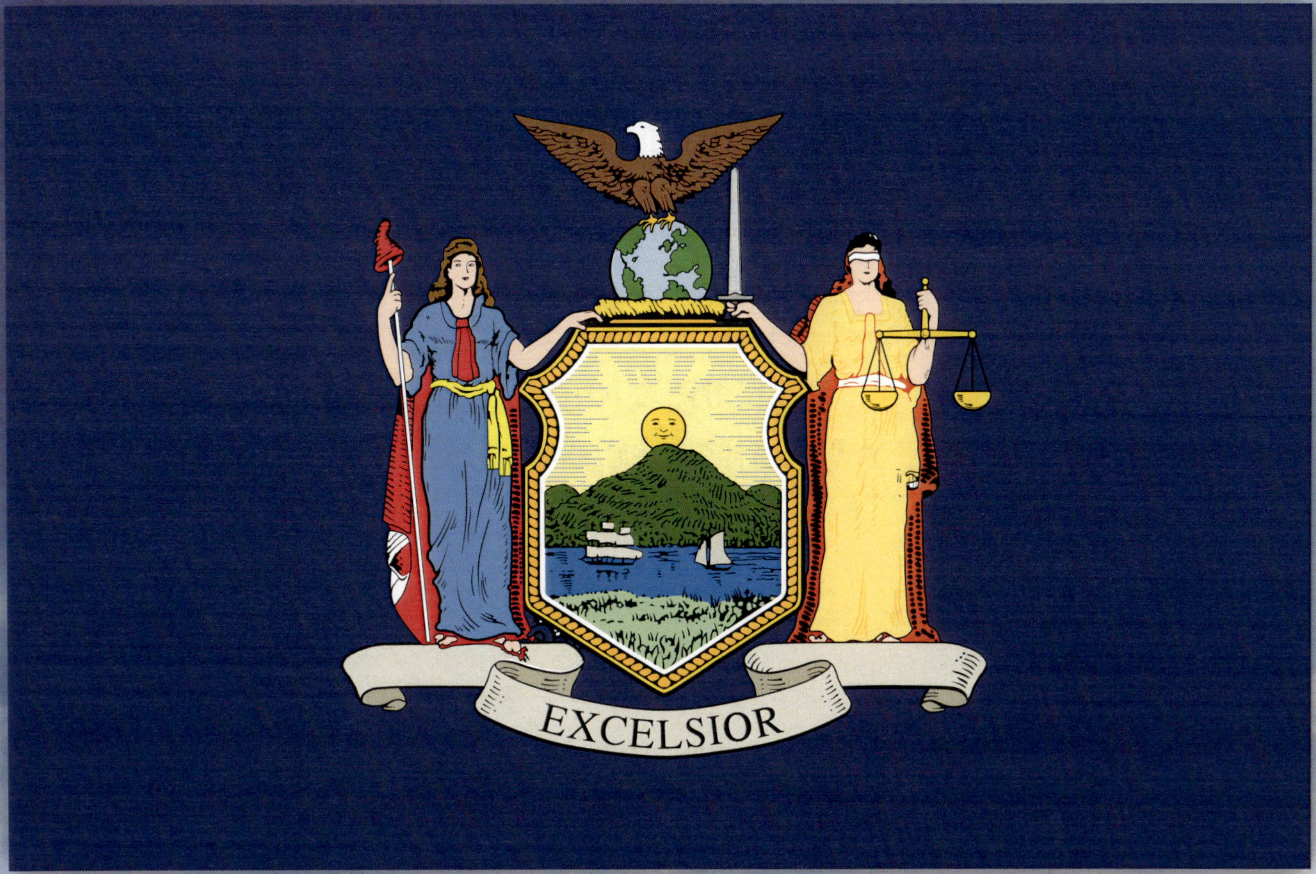
EXCELSIOR

CAPITAL

Say hello to Albany,
the capital city of New York!

There is an important building in Albany.
It is the State Capitol.
New York's laws are made there!

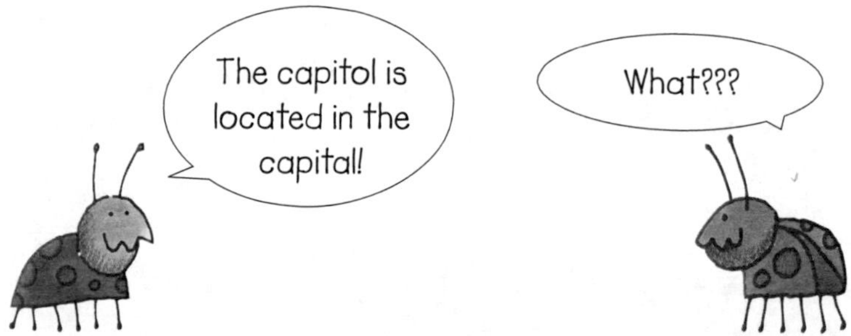

Capitol

SEAL

I am a seal,
but I am not the State Seal.
If I were, I would be very important.
I would be stamped on many official papers.
(Ouch, that might hurt!)

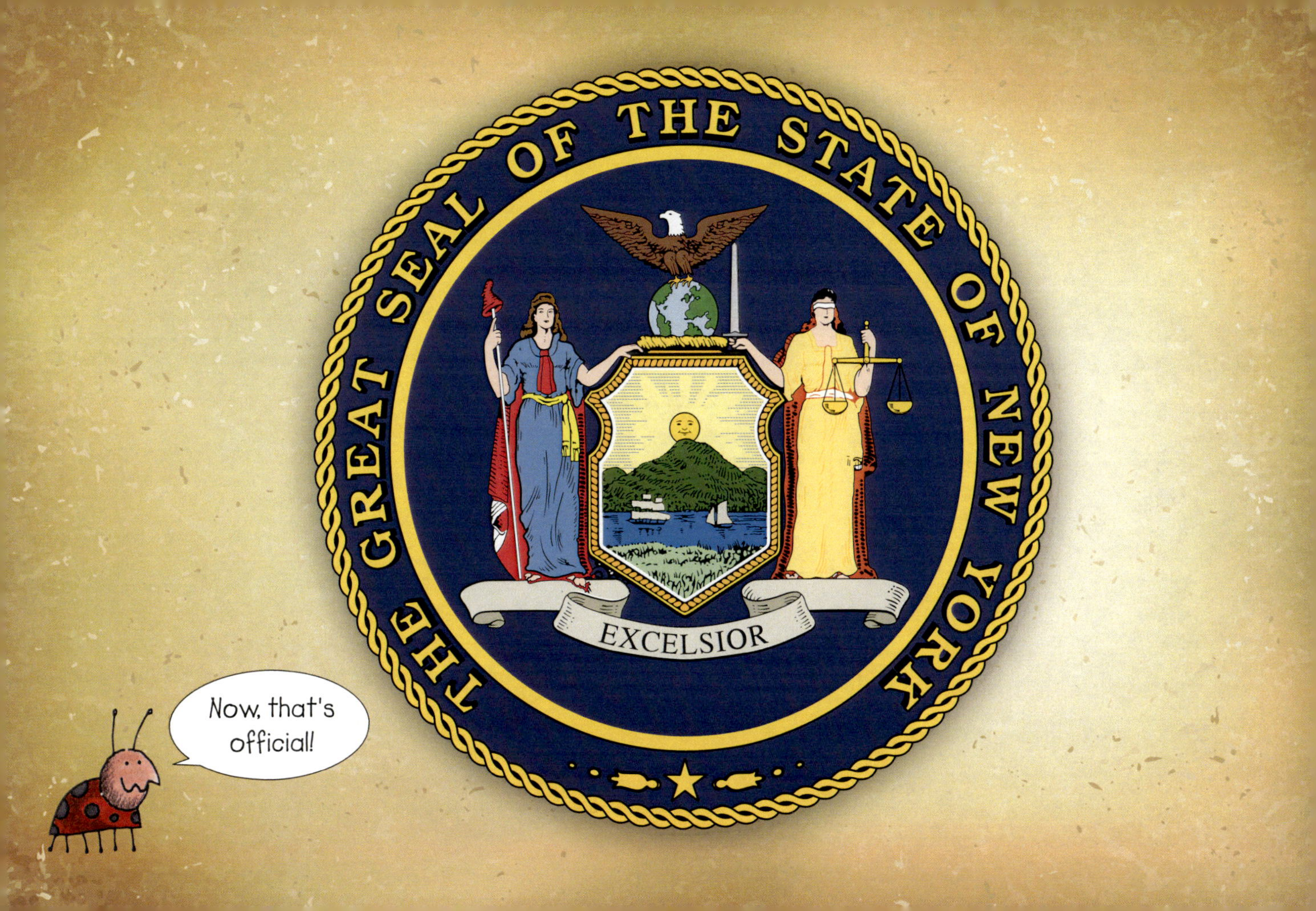
THE GREAT SEAL OF THE STATE OF NEW YORK
EXCELSIOR
Now, that's official!

NICKNAME

State nicknames are fun!
State nicknames are great!
They share fun facts
about each state!

New York's nickname is "The Empire State."

The Empire State Building is in New York City!

The Empire State

BORDERS

New York is in a region called "the Northeast."

New York borders five other states.
It also borders the country of Canada.
Find New York and its neighbors on the map!

Borders

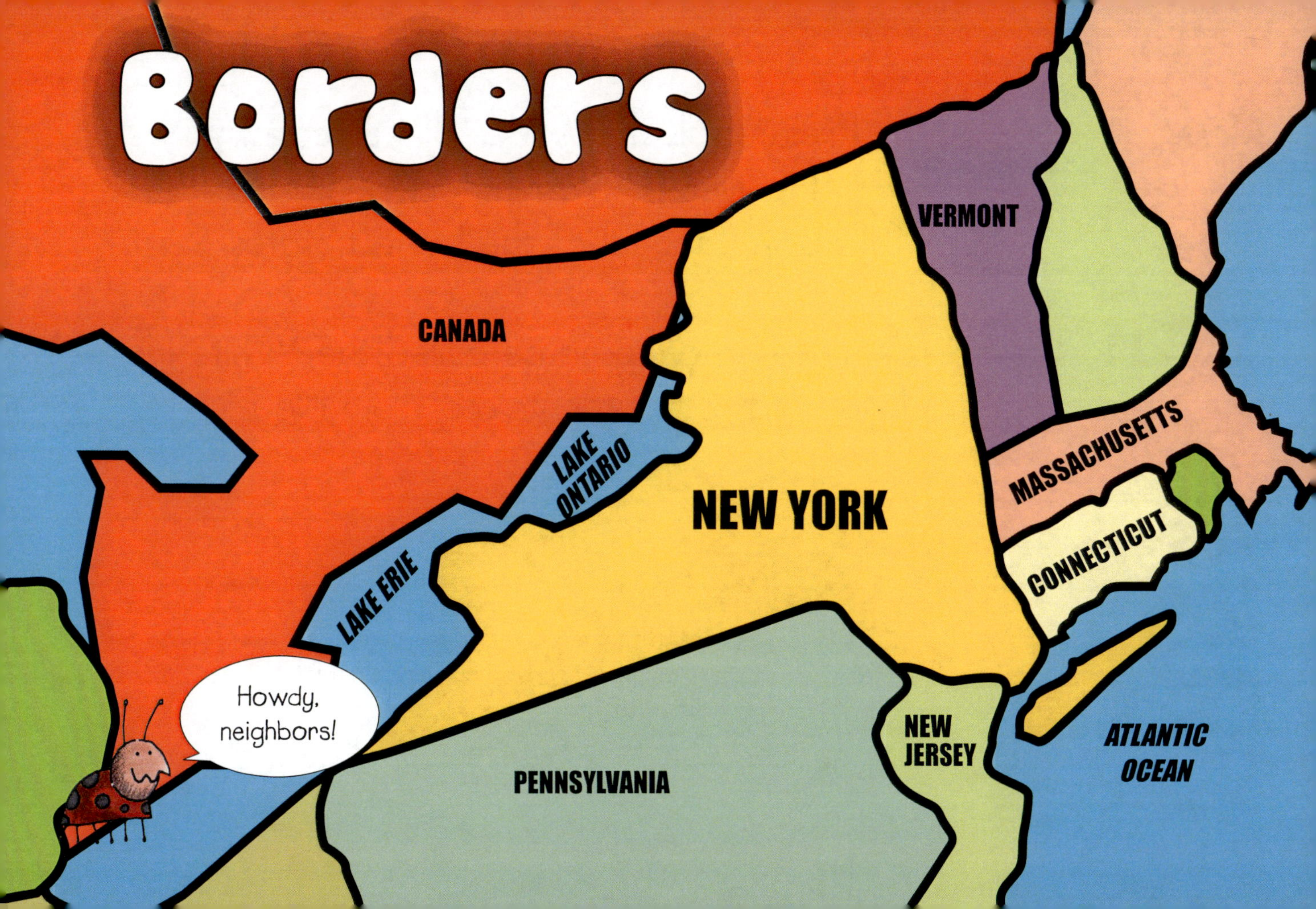
CANADA
VERMONT
LAKE ONTARIO
NEW YORK
MASSACHUSETTS
CONNECTICUT
LAKE ERIE
Howdy, neighbors!
NEW JERSEY
ATLANTIC OCEAN
PENNSYLVANIA

PRESIDENT

The President is the leader of our country.
He lives in Washington, D.C.
That is the capital of the United States.

The President lives in a big house called the White House.
Six United States Presidents are from New York!

Martin Van Buren
8th President
Millard Fillmore
13th President
Chester A. Arthur
21st President
Grover Cleveland
22nd and 24th
President
Theodore Roosevelt
26th President
Franklin D. Roosevelt
32nd President

PEOPLE

Many famous people

Elizabeth Cady Stanton

Leader of the early women's rights movement

George Eastman

Changed photography by inventing the Kodak camera and rolled film

John D. Rockefeller

Entrepreneur who started the Standard Oil Company

call our state home!

PEOPLE

Eleanor Roosevelt

First Lady and wife of President Franklin Roosevelt

Maurice Sendak

Writer and illustrator who wrote *Where the Wild Things Are*

Michael Jordan

NBA player said to be one of the best basketball players of all time

Eastern Bluebird

I am the state bird, and I fly
over New York, proud and high.

As I fly, up in the sky,
I flap my wings to tell you "Hi!"

The New York state bird is the Eastern Bluebird.

BIRD

Rose

FLOWER

I am the Rose.
I am the state flower.

I grow where it's warm and sunny.
I climb over shrubs and walls.
I help make New York beautiful!

Look at me! Smell me!
But don't touch my sharp thorns!

Sugar Maple

TREE

I am a Sugar Maple—I'm the state tree.
All over New York is where to find me.

My roots run deep, they keep me strong.
I can live for hundreds of years—that's very long!

I stand up straight, big and tall.
Don't climb too high—it would hurt to fall!

Ladybug

INSECT

I am the Ladybug
I am the state insect.

I am a type of beetle.
I am red with black polka dots!

Gardeners and farmers love me.
I eat bugs off their plants.
I help New York crops grow.

Atlantic Ocean

BEACHES

Let's go to the beach!

We can swim in the waves.
We can play in the sand.

We can build a big castle
where water meets land.

New York's beaches are home to many animals:

Sea Turtles **Fish** **Birds** **Crabs** **Dolphins** **and More!**

Adirondack Mountains

MOUNTAINS

New York's Adirondack Mountains are
the place to be.
Hiking, fishing, camping—
fun for you and me.

Winter weather brings lots of snow.
Temperatures drop to freezing and below!

Rivers

RIVERS

New York has many rivers.
People like to use them
for boating and fishing!

This habitat is home to many animals:

Birds Deer Snakes Frogs Fish and More!

Early settlers used New York's rivers for trade and travel.
Rivers were New York's first highways!

Statue of Liberty

LANDMARK

The Statue of Liberty is a large statue
in New York City!
It was a gift to the United States from France.
It is a national monument!
The statue is a symbol of freedom.

The Statue of Liberty sits on its own island.
It is called Liberty Island.
The island is in New York Harbor.

New York Crops

AGRICULTURE

New York has many farms.
Why?
Because New York has good soil and a mild climate!

Some of the top crops grown in New York include:

Hay **Corn** **Apples** **Potatoes**

Hey!
Don't forget about me!
I am a New York cow.
I produce lots of milk to make dairy products!

Mooooooooo!

Sports in New York

SPORTS

Baseball! Basketball! Football! Hockey!
New York has it all.

Whether you like to watch or play,
You are sure to have a ball!

Mets **Yankees** **Knicks**

Bills **Giants**

Jets **Rangers**

Islanders

Sabres **& More!**

New York: Home of New York City

CLAIM TO FAME

New York City is the biggest city in the United States! It is home to many businesses and famous landmarks.

Many people say New York City is the most exciting city in the world!

Many immigrants came to New York City to make a new life in America!

GLOSSARY

climate: weather conditions in an area over a long period of time

elect: to choose someone by voting

habitat: a place where plants or animals naturally live

immigrant: a person who moves to a new country

laws: rules made by the government

monument: a statue or building built to remember a person or event

region: an area that has similar characteristics

settlement: the first community in an area